AF614947

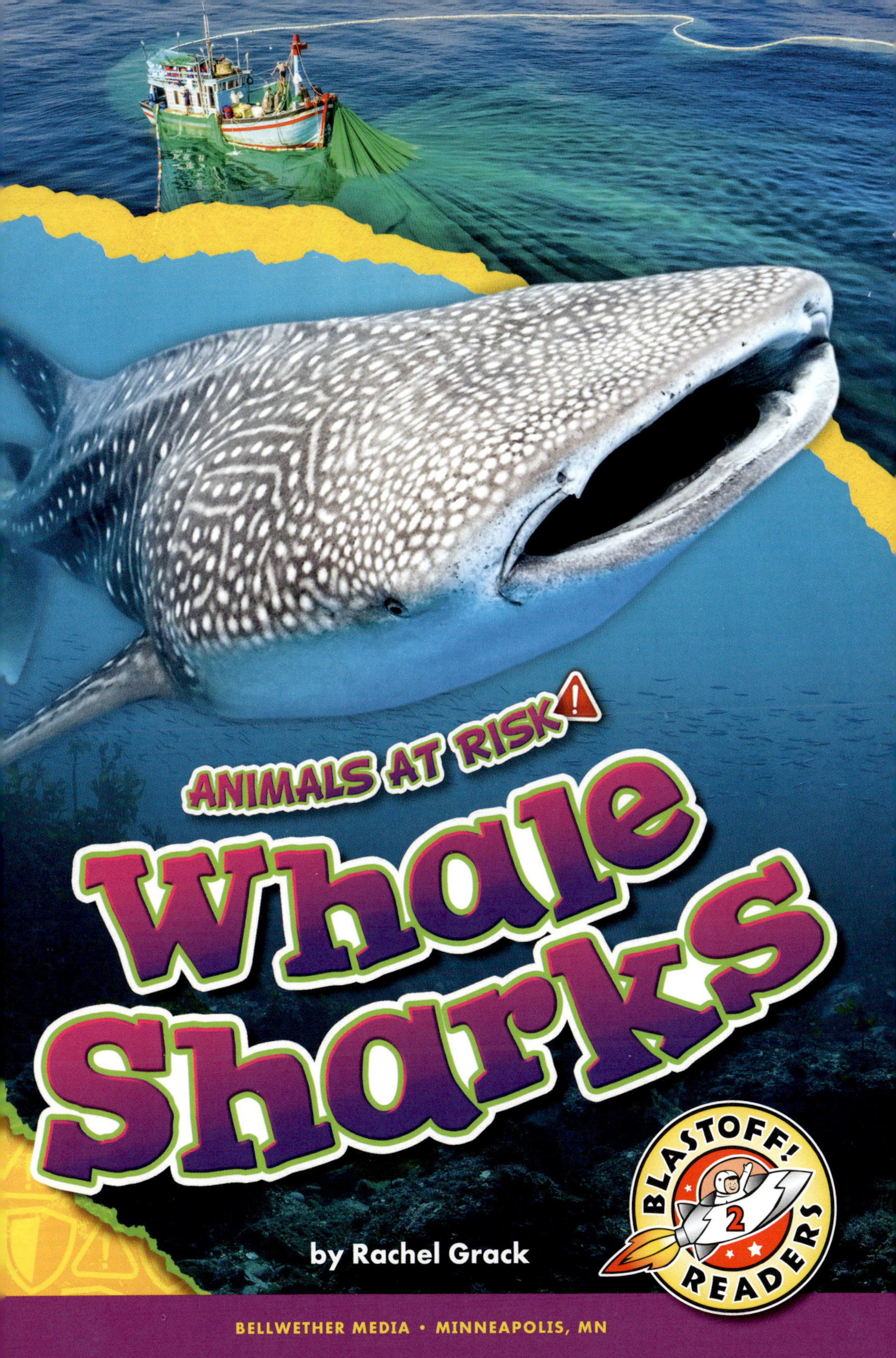
ANIMALS AT RISK
Whale Sharks
by Rachel Grack
BLASTOFF! 2 READERS
BELLWETHER MEDIA • MINNEAPOLIS, MN

Blastoff! Readers are carefully developed by literacy experts to build reading stamina and move students toward fluency by combining standards-based content with developmentally appropriate text.

LEVELS

Level 1 provides the most support through repetition of high-frequency words, light text, predictable sentence patterns, and strong visual support.

Level 2 offers early readers a bit more challenge through varied sentences, increased text load, and text-supportive special features.

Level 3 advances early-fluent readers toward fluency through increased text load, less reliance on photos, advancing concepts, longer sentences, and more complex special features.

★ **Blastoff! Universe**

Reading Level

Grade K

Grades 1–3

Grade 4

This edition first published in 2025 by Bellwether Media, Inc.

Library of Congress Cataloging-in-Publication Data

LC record for Whale Sharks available at: https://lccn.loc.gov/2024009431

Editor: Kieran Downs Designer: Brittany McIntosh

Printed in the United States of America, North Mankato, MN.

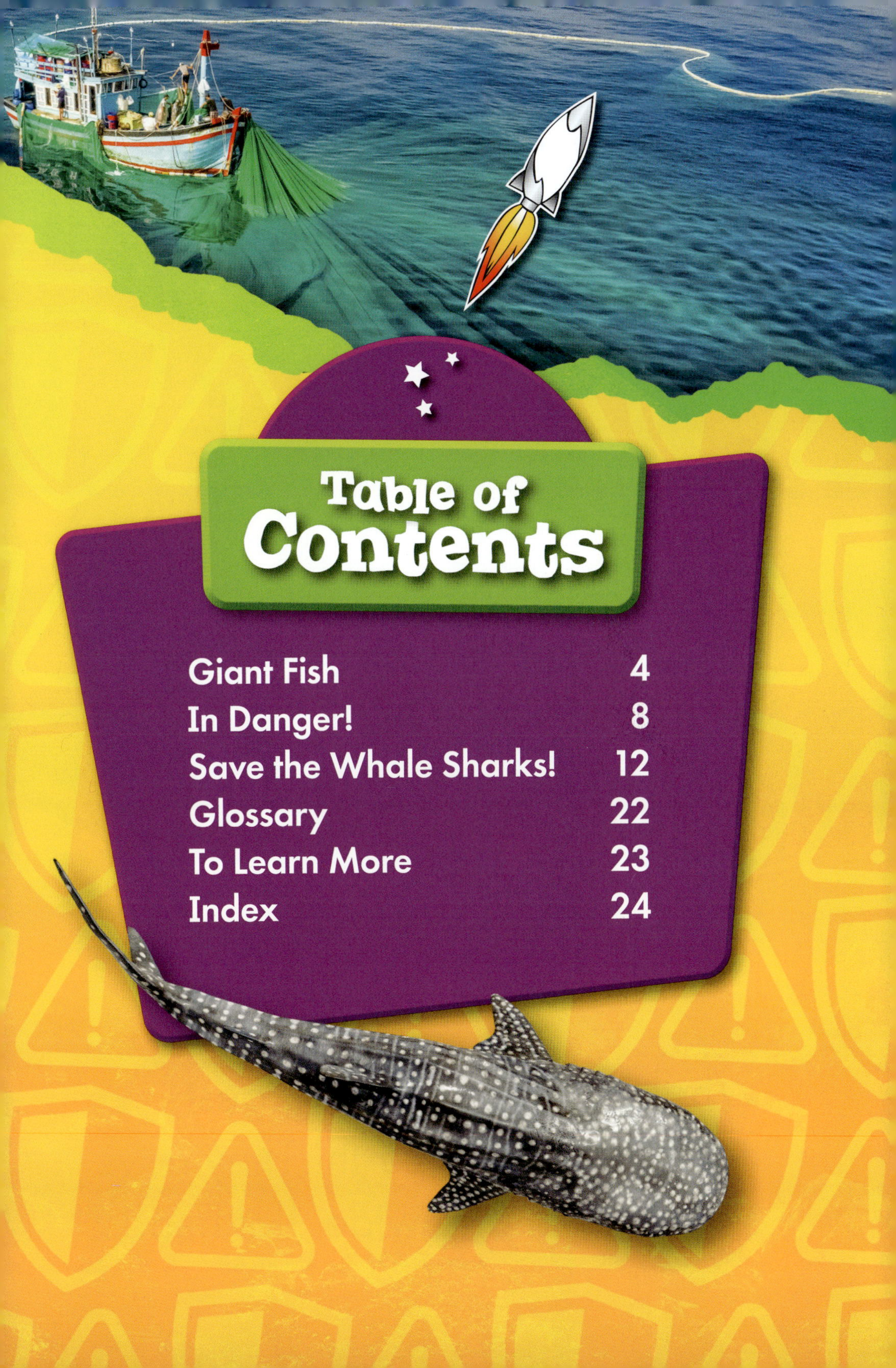

Table of Contents

Giant Fish

Whale sharks are the largest fish **species** on Earth! They have spotted skin and wide, flat heads.

They live in oceans
around the world.

Many whale sharks once traveled the oceans. They moved to different feeding grounds.

Today, whale sharks are **endangered**. People cause most of their problems.

In Danger!

Oceans are filled with **pollution**. Whale sharks swallow trash by mistake. **Climate change** also affects their food supply.

Boats pass through whale shark **habitats**. The boats can hit sharks.

Poachers hunt whale sharks for their liver oil and fins. Some people eat their meat.

Whale sharks also get caught in fishing gear.

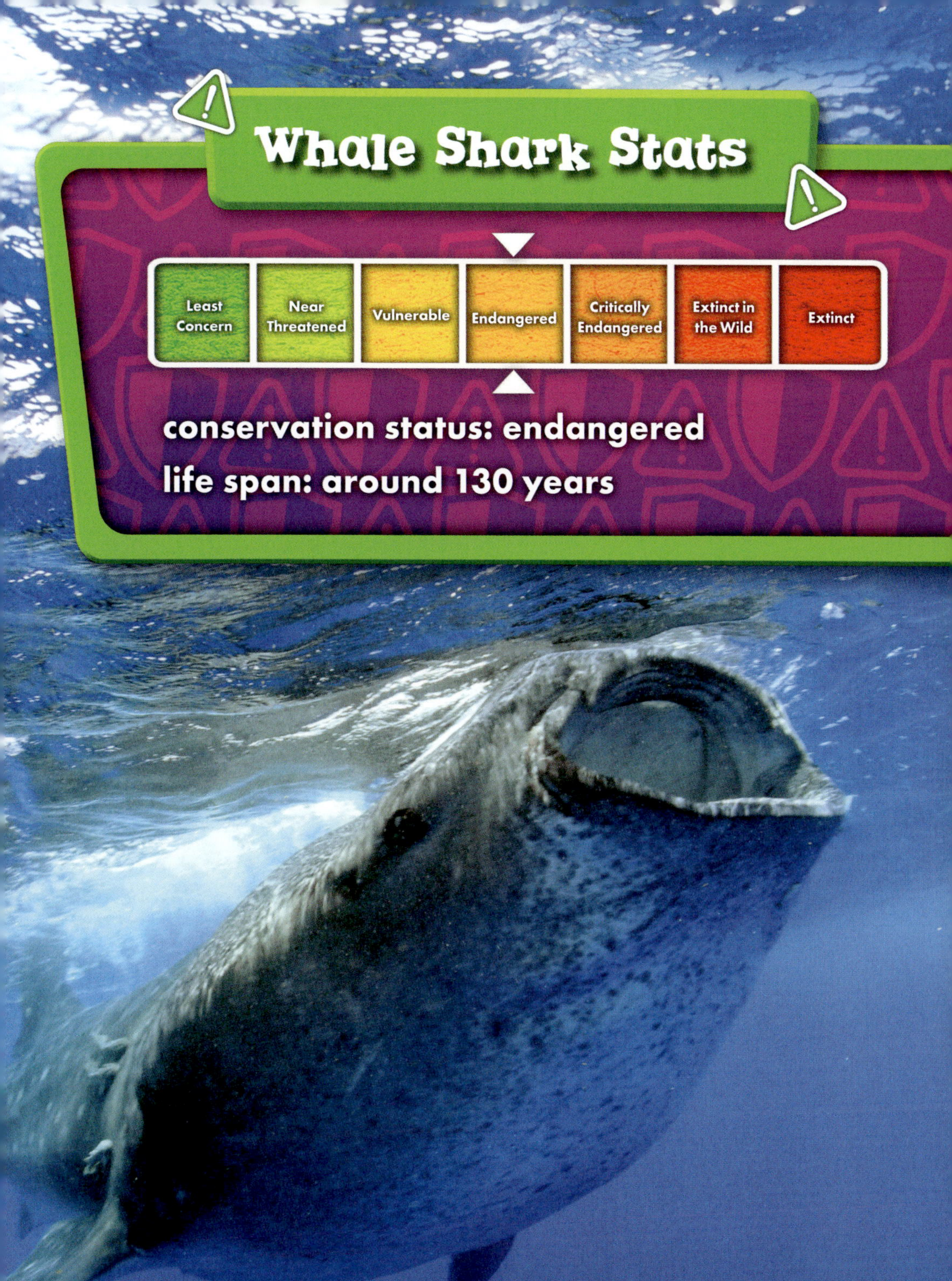

Whale Shark Stats

conservation status: endangered

life span: around 130 years

Save the Whale Sharks!

Whale sharks keep oceans healthy. Their poop puts **nutrients** into the water.

They also help control the number of **plankton** and small fish.

The World with Whale Sharks

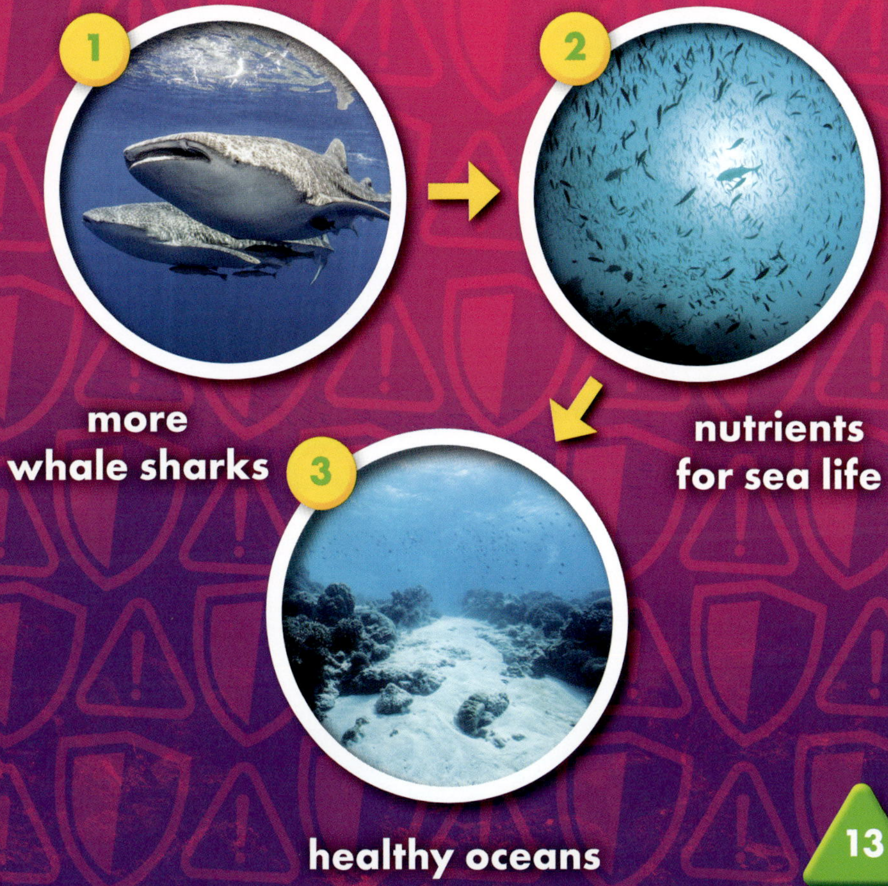

1 more whale sharks

2 nutrients for sea life

3 healthy oceans

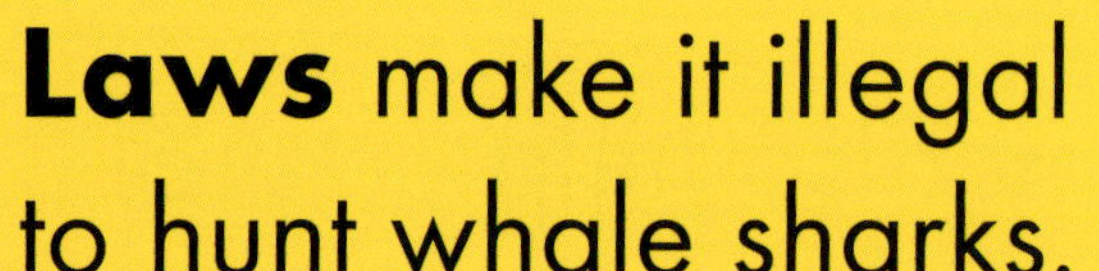

Laws make it illegal to hunt whale sharks.

Police work to catch poachers. They also stop people from selling shark meat.

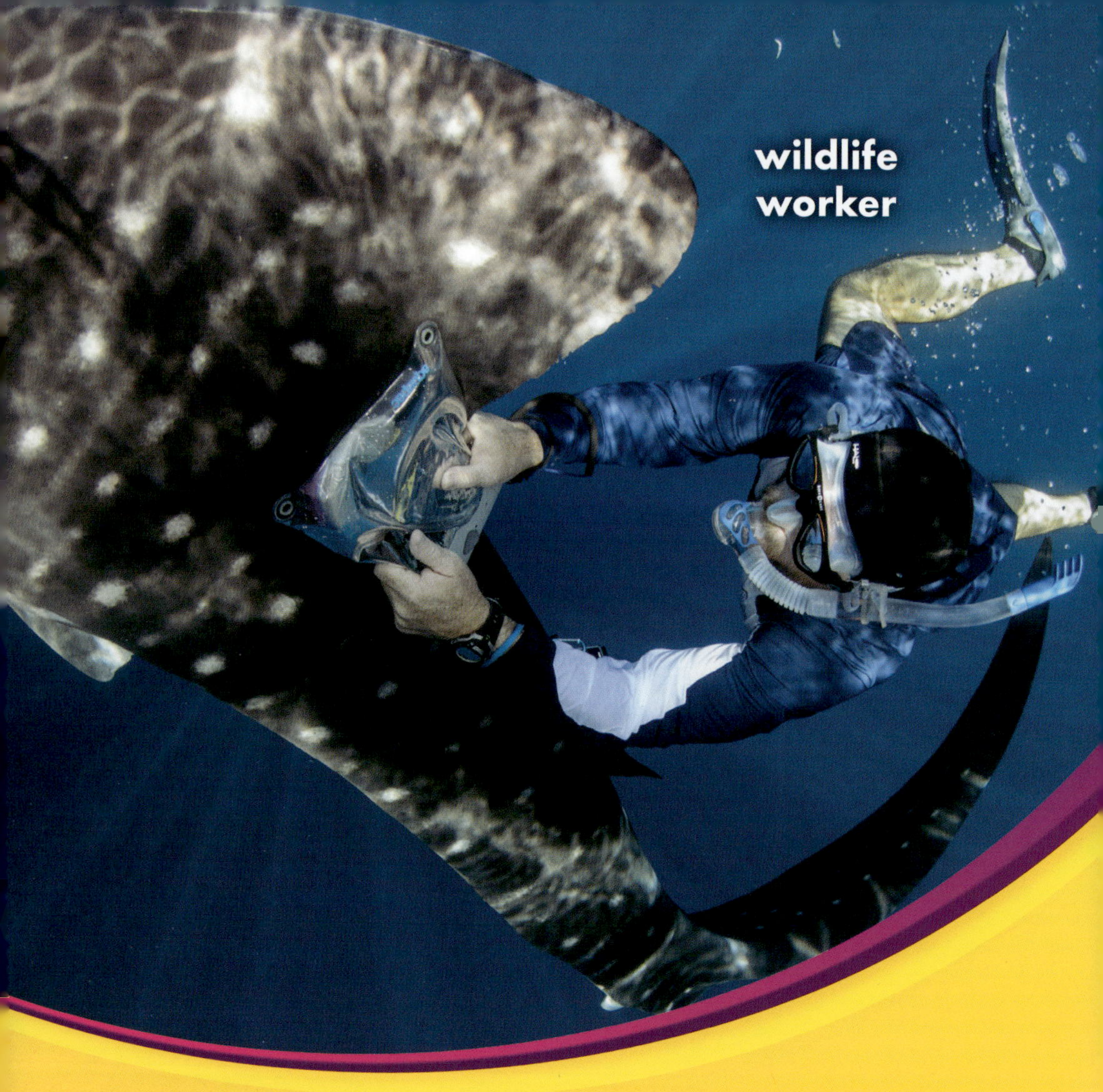

Wildlife workers use **technology** to track whale sharks. They learn about shark **migration paths** and habitats.

Large ships learn to avoid whale shark homes.

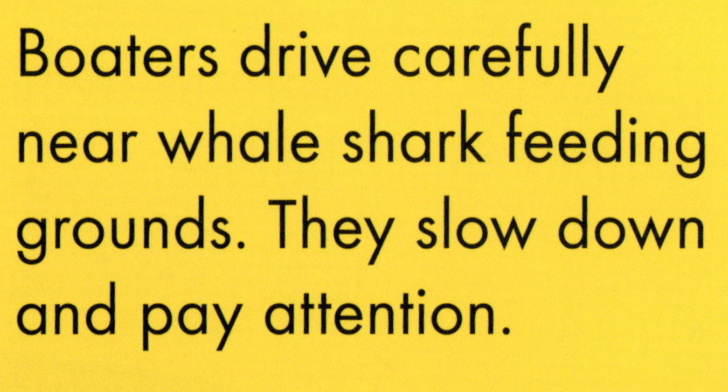

Boaters drive carefully near whale shark feeding grounds. They slow down and pay attention.

Divers watch whale sharks from a distance. People and sharks stay safe.

People can slow climate change by using less **energy**. Cleaning up beaches keeps trash out of oceans.

Together, everyone can save these ocean giants!

Glossary

climate change–a human-caused change in Earth's weather due to warming temperatures

endangered–in danger of dying out

energy–the power to make things work

habitats–the places where animals live

laws–rules that must be followed

migration paths–pathways used to travel from one place to another, often with the seasons

nutrients–things needed by people, animals, and plants to stay strong and healthy

plankton–ocean plants or animals that drift in water; most plankton are tiny.

poachers–hunters who catch or harm animals illegally

pollution–substances that make nature dirty; pollution usually comes from humans.

species–kinds of animals

technology–tools created by science used to make and share useful things or to solve problems

To Learn More

AT THE LIBRARY

Golusky, Jackie. *Whale Sharks: Nature's Biggest Fish.* Minneapolis, Minn.: Lerner Publications, 2024.

Humphrey, Natalie. *Whale Shark: Enormous Fish.* Buffalo, New York, N.Y.: PowerKids Press, 2024.

Murray, Julie. *Whale Sharks.* Minneapolis, Minn.: Pop!, 2024.

ON THE WEB

FACTSURFER

Factsurfer.com gives you a safe, fun way to find more information.

1. Go to www.factsurfer.com.
2. Enter "whale sharks" into the search box and click 🔍.
3. Select your book cover to see a list of related content.

Index

The images in this book are reproduced through the courtesy of: crisod, front cover, p. 5; Nguyen Quang Ngoc Tonkin, front cover (tear), p. 3; AJONE, p. 3; EXTREME-PHOTOGRAPHER/ Getty, p. 4; weera bunnak, pp. 6, 17; Mark Carwardine, p. 8; Rich Carey, pp. 9 (left), 14; chatchai kusolsinchai, p. 9 (right); Mathieu Meur/ Stocktrek Images/ Getty, p. 9 (bottom); by wildestanimal/ Getty, p. 10; ArteSub/ Alamy, pp. 10-11; Rienhard Dirscherl/ Alamy, p. 12; wildestanimal, p. 13 (left); Ethan Daniels, p. 13 (right); littlesam, p. 13 (bottom); Animalgraphy, p. 15; SuperStock/ Pete Oxford/ Minden Pictures, p. 16; GUILLERMO ARIAS/ Contributor/ Getty, p. 18; Westend61 GmbH/ Alamy, p. 19; Alen thien, p. 20; Fata Morgana by Andrew Marriott, pp. 20-21; Andrea Izzotti, p. 23.